Kingdom Come

and Other Poems

Kingdom Come

and Other Poems

Don Gutteridge

Wet Ink Books

First Edition

Wet Ink Books
www.WetInkBooks.com
WetInkBooks@gmail.com

Kingdom Come and Other Poems
by Don Gutteridge

Cover Design – Richard M. Grove
Layout and Design – Richard M. Grove

Typeset in Garamond
Printed and bound in Canada
Distributed in USA by Ingram,
        — to set up an account — 1-800-937-0152

Library and Archives Canada Cataloguing in Publication

Title: Kingdom come : and other poems / Don Gutteridge.
Names: Gutteridge, Don, 1937- author.
Identifiers: Canadiana 20220408998 | ISBN 9781989786758 (softcover)
Classification: LCC PS8513.U85 K56 2022 | DDC C811/.54—dc23

Table of Contents

Part One:
Portraits of the Point

Part Two:
Kingdom Come

Part One

Portraits of the Point

Davy

Davy Sadler was the envy
of every impecunious
boy on the block, pushing
his blue, rubber-tired
bus or his blood-red
fire engine across
his Grandma's verandah,
while we watched from our perch in the
peasants' pew, and Davy's
mother would arrive once
a month on the dot from her Ottawa
eyrie, where she civilled as a servant,
to ask him what kind of toy
he might like next –
in lieu of a Dad.

Neil

Neil Barr – blond,
bronzed and beautiful –who swam
ten miles along the Lake
just to feel his bones
float, taught us all
to swim, and love our bodies
blissfully buoyant, and the girls
who gathered to watch his patient
tutelage wished he would whet
their whistle, but he had other
urges no village could abide
or leave unpurged, and so
we lost him to the mean streets
of Tinsel Town, where I hope
he found comfort with his kind.

Easton

Easton Burgess greeted
each customer at his grocery
door with a morning smile
(occasionally oiled by alcohol),
while his wife and daughter manned
the barricades behind, and whenever
Bob and I arrived
to buy some incidental
item, I was always
the Colonel and Bob the General,
and we got the royal salute
or the whiskey-assisted grin,
and we watched him lower the ice-
cream scoop into the vanilla
bin, give it an extra curl
or two and let it skid
to a plump stop, just
short of a double-dip –
because I think he liked
kids with their untroubled
love more than the elders
who drove him to drink.

A Wide Berth

My Gran warned me that whenever
I was walking to the beach,
I should give a wide berth
to the odd, green, flat-
roofed abode with the steamed
windows, barred doors
and humped hedges, that Burch
explained, *sotto vo*ce,
was a Turkish bath, where men,
too nude not to be
noticed, had their bellies
rubbed, while squatting in tiled
tubs like Sultans to let
the heat swivel their sweat
and blister their body, and even
though I lurked and looked
a lot, the only soul
I ever saw leaving the premises
was a neatly-suited gentleman
with a Bible under his arm
and a worried smile on his face –
as if he might be late
for his meeting with God.

Pool Room

My mother warned me off
the Pool Room, tucked in
behind the beige drapery
of Bill Barr's smoke-
shop, where Butch and I
sipped on tepid Pepsis
and wondered what kind of
comic lurked below
the counter in plain brown
wrappers, and served with a smirk
to middle-aged 'gents,"
or listened for the click of cue
and numbered balls, and the leathery
thwack of a well-sighted
shot hitting home,
and we imagined the sharks
and punters, all spit
and swagger, or feigning boredom
as they lit up with a fag just
rubbed between finger and thumb,
and O how I yearned to be
unyoung, to break every
righteous rule and smothering
taboo.

Over the River

Point Edward: 1946

Everything 'over the River'
was bigger and better: my American
uncle drove a brand-
new Buick, lived in a
four-bedroom bungalow,
drew a superintendent's
salary and mingled with Masons,
and when Gran got her twelve-
inch Westinghouse,
it was Howdy Doody we watched,
and Sid Caesar and *their*
Hit Parade and, once
a month, Eddie Cantor,
warbling 'I'm a Yankee
Doodle Dandy,' and I don't
recall exactly when I decided
to reinvent myself as a writer
and let my stories teem
with the people and places of my tiny
wayside town, and have
my poems dream them into being

The Need to Nosh

Point Edward: 1947

Two groceries graced
the main drag of my town:
O'Neil's and *Burgess Market,*
the former a nineteenth-century
edifice, two stories
tall, sturdied with red-clay
brick, and with windows
generous enough to welcome
light, set in a sculpted
stone skirt that greeted
the street honestly, while three
doors east the upstart
Burgess enterprise got
everyone's attention by burning
to the ground in a fury of flame,
smoke and charred tinder,
then rising again
like Lazarus on a good day,
with cinder-block walls
and a mustard-hued plastic
façade that set tongues
a-wagging and old-timers
into shock, and these two
shops – plain or posh,
it doesn't matter - satisfied
nicely our need to nosh.

Happy Butler

Happy Butler, seventy-
years young, plastered
badly, slathering the village
walls with a sort of alabaster
sludge, but he made the rounds
in a superannuated truck,
so coated with lime
it couldn't be seen in a fog,
accompanied always by his faithful
companion, a mutt of no
particular pedigree, and when
he came to Gran's to do
some patching, I watched him
wield his trowel with the ease
of Toscanini's baton,
and I knew what I wanted to be
when I got big enough
to drive a truck or deserve
a dog.

Herbie

Herbie Gilbert, each
weekday morning, would back
his Tin Lizzie, all
fumes and farts, onto the
flawed asphalt of our street,
and as he passed us, gawking
on the walk, he would lean on
his ooga-ooga horn,
as if to say, "Here I am
and life is a boogie-woogie
we dance till we dizzy!"
and we waved him on his way
from our perch on the curb, our joy
at being just "we" and alive
as buoyant as a bloom in the heart.

Long Tom

Long Tom Shaw
was so thin that if
he bent sideways to the sun,
he cast no shadow,
and each summer morning,
he would lope past my lemonade
on route to the freight-sheds,
tip his cap and drop a nickel
in the pot, and I often wondered
how that frail-seeming
frame could muscle a load
of lumber or shoal coal
among the thick-thumbed
stevedores, and when the snows
came and the Bay below us
froze over, I could see him,
from Gran's verandah, cutting
ice and boosting the big
blocks ashore, as if
they were merely flotsam and he:
right where he belonged.

Harry Fisher

Harry Fisher, veteran
of the Somme and other killing
grounds, occupied a stucco-ed
abode on the corner of Monk
and Michigan, his yard - front,
side and back – littered
with failed fridges, castaway
ranges, old stoves,
staggering in the sun, abandoned
beds with coiled springs
the wind whistled through,
a three-legged couch,
leaking innards, a baby-
buggy with no infant to hug,
and sundry other pepper-
pots and gimcrack crockery,
and any afternoon saw
Harry pacing the Main,
in search of something he could never
quite find – in the clutter
of his home or the maelstrom of his mind.

Warp

I'm pretty sure it was Wiz
who suggested a summer circus
and proffered a shady spot
for our single 'ring,' and a pair
of purloined pews for the cheap
seats, and kids came
from blocks around, bored
or curious or both - and the show
began with Gerry donning
his lion's duds (stitched
by his sister) and trying to put
more gruff in his growl
or paw more chair than air,
while Bones essayed to tame him
with a whip and a whistle (that wouldn't),
followed by prolonged (mock)
applause (and a whistle that did),
and Miss Withers arrived
with her prancing pups (who preferred
dithering to dance), and then
came the clowns - my brother
and I in Halloween garb,
happily taking pratfalls
for a clap or a laugh, and O
the cheers when somebody's teddy
dropped from aloft on the high-
wire Wiz had rigged, and stopped
on the knob of the nearest nose,
and whenever I'm beset by the 'glums'
or 'anything goes,' I just
recall that magic summer
and the warp of its wonder.

Jack

I don't know what draws
one person into the ambit
of another – something perhaps
about the way they stand
in their own stillness or a glint
in the glance, promising more,
or simply the feeling that aloneness
isn't bred in the bone,
but the day Jack Fulcher
arrived in my Grade Four,
I knew we'd be brothered,
and when I knelt beside him
in the far schoolyard,
his smile was a better beckoning
than any word of welcome
or heartfelt hello – and that night
I dreamt his life was in danger
and I came roaring to the rescue
like batman in full flight,
and I hugged him till his grin
gave up, and dreams are
hopes waiting to be
surmised, and so it was
that Jack and I travelled
in tandem all the way
to Grade Five.

Air Raid

When the Point Edward fire-
alarm severed the evening
peace with all the bluster
and blare of an air-raid
siren in the midst of the Blitz,
a half-dozen rubber-
suited denizens left
their supper untouched
or interrupted a post-
prandial snooze to make
their way by divers routes
to Station Number One
(of one), and leap like water-
logged frogs aboard
the brand-new hook-
and-ladder, already gassed
game, by which time
every ragamuffin, almost-
orphaned kid had also
arrived, and the whole cock-
eyed caravan sped
three blocks away
to where a grass fire,
impudently unablaze,
smouldered and died, while the fire
brigade, without hems or haws,
uncorked the water cannon –
to mock applause.

Rituals

In the mornings, it was Otis
Anderson who delivered our milk
in goose-necked bottles,
while his horse drew the wagon
with a slow, hooved plod,
rattling glass all the way,
who needed no prompt
– whistle or flick – to move
the cargo on to the next
paying customer (a nickel
tickling her empty on the porch),
following some equine Mercator
in its head and careful not
to drop its breakfast on Gran's
allotment; and in the afternoons
it was the iceman, wobbling
a-kilter down our walk,
the tonged ice gleaming
in his grip, while we trailed the drips
to the back of the truck for the
slivered chips that teased
on the tongue – and we were young
enough to think these daily
doings, these rituals of childhood
would last as long as we did.

Butch

Butch McCord, whose mother
rarely remembered calling him
by the name she'd given him,
was my best friend, who kept
the schoolyard bullies at bay
and let me win at marbles,
and when we moved to the country,
hopped aboard his two-
wheeler and followed us
and the van until we vanished
at the next bend, and I regret
to say I soon found
a new best bud – and the last
I heard of Butch: he had fathered
five sons, then left them be:
running full-sail
(from some inner din)

Gary: Walking the Walk

Gary McCord and my brother,
bob, donned my Gran's
cast-off frocks and low-
heeled pumps, and clumped
up and down the side-
yard walk, like a pair
of mincing models, sunning
them buns on the runway,
and no-one guessed that they were
gay, or cared what
secret selves they kept
furled in the closet and longed
to loose upon a gender-
bending world, and Gary
came out in Chicago and Bob
in Berne, where they groomed like grannies
and walked the walk.

Confectioner

Harry Brand, who hadn't seen
seventy for some time,
kept his *Confectionery* afloat
on the main drag with a selection
of baked goods: bread-
loaves fresh from the five-
o'clock oven (the flavour
woven in), and eclairs
topped aloft with chocolate,
and sugar-oozing strudel
(nothing more than dime),
but it was the sweets and candy
that drew every kid
who could walk a block to Harry's
shop: bubble gums,
and jawbreakers to gnaw on,
and blackballs (four for a penny)
and heart-shaped lozenges
that bespoke love and other
affections, and licorice cigars
and unlit cigarettes, and all-
day suckers we licked
till out tongues gave up,
and when we were shy of a nickel,
a two-cent grab-bag
would do, but most of all,
I think we liked the wink
in Harry's eye and the smile
he'd kept afloat for more than
seventy years.

Duffy

Ken "Duffy" Duffield
sported a set of buck
teeth that would have made
a beaver boast, that no
dentist could cure, and in
the schoolyard, whenever
he was teased he would grin the un-
ruffled grin he wore
like a buffoon's badge, and turn
away, until the day
he struck back with furious
fists, and we watched in awe
as he marched to the principal with both
palms up and held high,
and the slap of the strap, like the crack
of a whip on the victim's skin,
could be heard three rooms
down the hall, where we shuddered
with each shameful stroke,
and waited for the cry –that did not
come.

Wizardry

I never saw my Dad on skates,
but I see him now in these
faded news clippings
he's collected and pasted proudly
in the scrapbook of his halcyon
hockey days: a balletomane
on ice with stick wizardry
and puck hustle – and I can
hear the of his blades and feel
the soft surge of pent-up
power as he breaks clear
of the clutter, leans at his ease
and fires the winner – and this
is all I have left of the man
who could sing like Bing.
whistle Dixie in the dark
and strum a uke till it mewed,
who drowned his talent in drink
and died for trying, but I think
this will have to do.

.

Badge

My town was a nursery for nick-
names: Rip Kemslie,
Dolly Gordon, Long
Tom Shaw, Pussy
Carr, Silent George
Hendrie and half-a-dozen
Shorties or Slims (who wished
to be otherwise), and my uncles
were baptized by our resident
part-time parsons
as Potsy and Iggy, and my Dad
answered only to Gubs
and my brother to Googie, and O
how I yearned, like my pals
Wiz and Butch, to be blessed
with some sobering sobriquet,
but the nearest I came to this
badge of belonging was a second
cousin calling me Duck,
but it didn't click, and I soldiered
on, as best I could,
as Don.

Dolly

Point Edward: 1947

Dolly Gordon, who lived
just two doors down,
worked up a worthy sweat
at the Freight Sheds in the
heathen heat of that summer
and cooled his jets in the
Bal-mor-al with buckets
of beer and toasts to fellow
tossers, and when he connived
to crawl his way home,
the missus was standing on the stoop,
skillet in hand and ready
to go, and Dolly, ever
the gentleman, doffed his cap
to let it land a better blow.

Silent George

Silent George Hendrie
believed a tongue was for talking
and his did: loud, long
and lusty: and when he'd thrown
the last switch on the afternoon
shift, he woiuld settle down
in the bunkhouse and unspool
a yarn about the thisness
of that or his glory days
riding the rails and dodging
bulls, and though the tale
was twice-told, it still
got a laugh where a laugh
was due, and I often heard him
whistling his way home, all
the stories-yet-to-be-yarned
dancing in his head.

Wiz

My pal Wiz, whose mother
insisted on calling him Dave,
was the captain of our small cabal,
and earned that sobriquet because
there wasn't a gizmo he couldn't
fizz or a gadget he couldn't
rachet into action, and his prize
pony was a derby-racer,
confected out of borrowed
buggy wheels and abandoned
boards, and lacquered as black
as Satan's ass, and we pushed him
around town, like a royal
in a rickshaw, from buffed
boulevard to grassy patch –
to the astonished applause of
passers-by and jaw-dropping
awe of denizens too dazzled
to wave, and when that storied
day wound down, I was pleased
to have basked in the glory-reflected
by do-it-all Dave.

Part Two

Kingdom Come

Kingdom Come

The Reverend Bell believed
in Predestination,
that God chose which souls
to savour, and he was pretty
certain to be among
the Elect, especially after
reaching his empty house
one day and, suspecting gas,
fumbled for a match, watched
it kindle in the dark – and wasn't
blown to Kingdom Come:
landing, instead, bouche bé
on his neighbour's grass, as blackened
as a skid-row bum

Ever and Anon

From my sick-bed below
the window, I could see
Missus Bray's straw
bonnet, and for a moment
I thought she was afloat
on her flowers, but when she bent
to bless a bloom, awed
perhaps by its petalled power,
or noticed the bees unseething
as they settled on the breeze – she was
herself again, ever
and anon, and something akin
to magic that day had come
and gone.

Muppetry

For Tom in loving memory

Supper was a hurried affair
when the Muppets were due
at six on the dot, and I loved
the luff of your laughter when Fozzie
Bear's homespun humour
and misanthropic monologues
fell flat, and how indignant
you got when the Critics, from the lofty
loges, heckled and otherwise
mocked the show and its shenanigans,
or giggled at Miss Piggy's
romantic antics, or chuckled
when the Swedish chef mangled
the language, and we held our breath
till Kermit arrived with his frog-
on-a-log croak and bugaboo
eyes, and entertained the troupe
with the vim of a failed vaudevillian,
and we imagined the puppeteers
crouched, unseen, below:
Ozz with his wizard fingers
and Jim, laughing himself
to death.

Giggles

For Bonnie and Sharon Lauer

The sisters Laur couldn't
take their eyes off
our banty rooster, preening
in his pen with his blood-red
cockade, and when he boosted
himself above an available
hen with an exquisite squeeze
of lid and larynx and a joyous
jiggle of his jousting rig,
they let their giggles bubble
up and their hair down.

Disguises

When I was a lad not quite
in my prime, before blue
jeans, minis or the lissome
leotard, girls disguised
their personal parts in divers
ways: skirts that flirted
with the hip but ballooned to the knee;
blouses with padded bras
that muted the loot they housed;
one-piece suits with the modesty
crotch; but nothing could stop us
from dreaming aloud about dimpled
domains or bulges that wowed,
or girls who seldom gave us
the time of day or paused
long enough to break
a heart.

What We Had In Mind

For Kate

When we christened you "Catherine"
and then called you "Kate,"
the neighbours thought of "Kiss-me-
Kate," or the Bard's subdued
shrew or Catherine the Great
with her hair down, or the fluttering
stutter of "K-K-Katie"
at her kitchen door, and my mother-
in-law took some months
to let it trickle off her tongue,
but whatever we might've had in mind,
you grew into your name and made it
known, in the world's eyes,
as your own, and no-one, empress
or not, dare dub you
otherwise.

News

My Gran scanned the pages
of the *News of the World* from front
to back and back again,
and left it intact on the kitchen
table, where I, just happening by,
pounced upon its pornographic
pablum, in which girls too
dozy to dodge were always
'interfered with' (or not),
and English crime took
three columns and a
                    skinful of ink to satisfy
the prurience of a grateful nation,
but, alas, my fantasies (though leering)
were fuzzy, and no-one thought
to let me know what
'interfering' was.

Blissful Wishing

For Sandy

Your Mum and Dad weren't
quite sure what to make
of me, three years
your senior and you in the
first bloom of your womanhood,
but whenever we cuddled on your living-
room couch, they,
all tact and trust, kept
discreetly distant, knowing
that young love like ours
was more blissful wishing
than bodily contact.

Lute

For Tom in loving memory

I wanted to vary the song
that would sing you softly to sleep,
reaching deep into my repertoire
 of lullaby lyrics for something
other than: "O the great ships
sail thru the Alley, Alley O"
and more like "Oh Dear"
of "Way Down Upon,"
but you insisted on your slumber-
inducing ditty, and by the time
I'd come to: "On the *first*
day of Sep-*tem*-ber,"
you'd be dallying your dreams:
my voice, like the thrum of a
lover's lute, still embering
there.

Wrought

When God fashioned Adam
and added Eve as an after-
thought, he must have known
the plot would see Adam
nt a pea in Eve's pod
and the nuptialled couple no longer
need His holy seed
to collude and propagate,
or feel obliged to keep
the Garden untarnished
by Time or turpitude,
and thus was a paradise lost
and a new world wrought.

On Listening To Robert Frost
Read His Poetry

First of all, there's the voice:
as if it's been run through a thresher
and re-assembled with a rustic
touch to season his bucolic
drawl, and then the poems:
so seeming simple, of everyday
happening, like apple-picking
aftermath and wooded roads
not taken and fences mended
friendly and hired men
in lieu of heroes, and these
verses with their homespun
couplets and understated
stamina will open our eyes
to the ways of wonder, and leave us
that much wiser.

Solace

O how I remember
those wintry rides
to school in Max's tinpot
"taxi," me in front,
hoping for heat, the sisters
Laur cozied in the back
with my brother, the windows
fringed with filigrees of frost,
the washboard road
juddering below, the over-
night snows dozing
on either side, and I wondered,
even then, if such
iconic moments would find
a privileged place in my mind
or seek some solace
in the purging words of a poem.

Scraps

For my father in loving memory

When you failed Grade Eight
for the third time (all that
scrambled grammar and words
estranged on the page), you must have
thought the world didn't want you
in it, but you'd already found
your skating legs and a rink
big enough to take you
in stride, and here in the scrapbook
you kept for me to find,
your name leaps from headlines
in bold New Roman:
of goals scored and last-
minute winners and hat-trick
magic and trophies won
for the home-town fans –
and no-one cared you hadn't yet
read *War and Peace,* for you wrote
your own biography in the
blood and blade of your game.

Bardic in the Bone

Once again, I find myself
alone in the green womb
of Grandfather's yard,
where bees, honey-drugged,
doze, and dream of clotted
combs in queen-sized
hives, and from the elderly
elm, leaning low:
the raucous caw of crows,
and on the dew-splashed
grass, Robin bobs
for breakfast and lets his song
throb, and it is here
I feel once again
something break and bloom –
bardic in the bone.

Peregrine

When I can no longer compose
poems to keep my soul
alive, when my muse has become
unenthused, like a rose
in limpid light, when my last
simile has sung itself out,
and I have just enough breath
to breathe a metaphor that might
uplift or move, I'll say
goodbye to loping tropes
and rhyming schemes, put down
my peregrine pen, and drift
like a dream to my death.

Wide-Eyed

For Tom in loving memory

And you: not yet seven,
standing in wide-eyed
wonder as I turn the volume up
to let the decibels dance,
and clutching my make-believe
baton like a tortured Toscanini,
conduct Beethoven's Ninth
as if Ludwig himself
were in the room and cheering
me on, and I wanted so much
to have you see how music
can move through muscle and blood
and set the mind in melodious
motion, and when the Daughters
of Elysium finally soar
their choric song into silence,
I see your toe tapping
and something in your eye
began to prance.

Debonaire

For Sandy

O how I yearned for a
girl-friend, someone
to hold my hand as if
it mattered, and cuddle or kiss
perhaps when the evening ebbed,
then you arrived with your blue-
eyed gaze, parked on my arm
and letting me stroll you
thru our streets like a strutting
panjandrum, like a beau
with his summer love in tow.

The Unfurling

These bulbs have weathered
Winter and its chaste chill,
curled in the grudging grip
of the ground, hoarding the heat
they sucked from the last lick
of Summer sun to keep
the tulip-womb warm
and the daffodil drey
abaft and bracing for bloom –
and when April rains arrive
to drench and lip-tickle,
something too young
to breathe seethes inside
and lets a world unfurl.

The Show

Chatham, Ontario: 1952

On lazy, hazy afternoons,
when I was still happy
enough to be young, we ran
the bases like proto-pros,
shagging flies that hung
in the above like a lover's swoon
and found their gulp in a glove,
or fielding grounders with their hap-
hazard non-stop hop,
and I always preferred to be pitcher,
watching the curl of my curve
outwit the lopsided lash
of the batter, and I dreamed of making it
big, of "going to the Show" -
back then: when there was nothing
more to know and dreams
were all we had to seem

Tea Service

Upstairs, tea was forbidden
fare, but below, where Gran
ruled the realm, tea was
taken with ceremonial flair
in bone-china cups
so thin you could see
you chin shimmering on the
other side, and O how I
loved its steaming, golden
glide from spout to the wee
splash of milk already
there, and two spoons
of sugar, sifting, to sweeten
the tooth, and what a joy
it was to be sipping on something
blissfully illicit, banned
above, and served with a
grin from Gran.

Luminous

For Marybelle Cooper

When Marybelle Cooper drapes
her new-found curves
(twin doves dozing
at bay in her tartan) over
our picket fence in the
luminous June light,
and when she beguiles me
her shy-sly smile,
my breath quickens, my heart
giddies and my senses swim,
and though I'd yet to discover
what love was (or the gist
of lust for that matter),
I think I just did.

At Last

When at last we got
a car, and Dad no longer
walked the mile from work,
we cared not that it was a
rusted-out rattletrap
that burned more oil than gas
and had to be cranked alive,
or that the diver's-side
window wouldn't mind its manners,
or that the doorknobs wobbled
before they caught, or the clutch
was weary of the gears, for we
were just thankful to be
on the road, like rievers on a roll,
and kicking up dust – and my Dad:
behind the wheel with a smile
on his face as wide as a
dealer with an ace in the hole.

Whistling Dixie

There wasn't a lusty lad
in the village who wouldn't
whistle for Dixie Dunham,
the raven-haired beauty
whose Dad raised a chestnut
sulky racer he kept tucked
in a little barn, where it could
preen for us if we happened by,
and whenever I stared at Dixie
as she walked the great gelding
onto the course and let it
shake its mighty mane
at the two-dollar punters,
I wasn't sure which I liked better:
the girl or the horse.

Ambient: Cameron Lake – 1990

For Tom in loving memory

With you in the bow and me
abaft, we lie in the amber
arms of the afternoon, and when
the sun is too soothing
on your brow, you let your line
go limp – and around us:
the lake, undimpled
and bracingly blue, dreaming
of itself perhaps or the fathoms
napping, ambient, below,
and this is how grace begins
and our love, like the lake,
gathers and brims.

Her Lapdog Eyes

For John

I well remember the day
our Scottie decided to go
for a skate instead of a walk,
and watched, in pedigreed shock,
as the ice gave way beneath
her skidding paws and invited
her in for a wintry swim,
and you, with no thought
but the life of your canine
companion, strode into the
watery waste, plucked up
her soggy deadweight,
tucked her, trembling, under
your coat, and trotted home
slowly to let her breathe
your body-heat and keep
her heart hiccupping, and there
you sat with her, cocooned
in your arms, until at last
she was warm enough to thank you
with her loving, lapdog eyes.

January Moon

For my mother in loving memory

You had just turned twenty
when you worried me into the world,
your wedding: hastily arranged
on foreign terrain, where a license
was easy on the dollar, your diamond:
a chip some gimcrack jeweller
jettisoned – and the young luminary
you worshipped from the moment you spied him
inkling in a rink and skating
like a bird in feathered flight,
barely old enough to vote,
but bathed in the raucous applause
of the hometown arbiters,
and you must have made love
under a January moon
in the star-harbouring dark,
but I bloomed too soon
in the womb, and soit was
we rode eight months
in tethered felicity, and when
I was born, you brushed my bard's
brow with your loving lips
and let me be me.

You Have a Daughter

For Kate

The nurse is clutching something
bundled that brings the smile
she beams at me, announcing
to me and the room, "You have a
daughter," and eases back
the blanket enwombing whatever's
cocooning within, but I notice
nothing but the blue hue
of the eyes, surprised to have arrived,
here or anywhere, but keeping
an appraising gaze glued
to mine, as if perhaps
we'd never said goodbye,
and when I spot the cinnamon
tufts haloing her brow,
my heart lurches in its ribbed
socket with such felicitous
fury, I know only that this
is the love that binds – bone
to bone.

Idling

For Marybelle, again

Coop and I, idling
on Canatara, one
eye on the wind-lashed
waves breaking on the
shoreline in foamed fury
and the other on Cousin Marybelle
and her one-piece chum,
letting the sun-hugged
sand nuzzle the hummocks
and hillocks of their just-come
curvature, and the lust they lit,
like a bride's bite, no jury
would indict.

The Day Wiz Vanished

Each summer morning
when I was free to be alive,
I made a beeline for Wiz's,
ever tinkering in his father's
cluttered shop, but one day
I found him gone from the usual
post, and his sister, from her wide
verandah, sighed and said,
"He's run off with the Burgess girl,"
and sure enough, when I finally
arrived on the scene, he was waltzing
arm-in-arm with curvy
Marlene and her wind-tossed
locks, and when I waved,
he essayed to rearrange his gaze,
but it was already lost
to other urges.

Swat Team

In the swelter of that summer season,
whenever I opened Gran's
verandah door to let the heat
breathe, the kitchen would be
a-buzz with house-flies
the size of baptized bats,
and Gran would seize the flit-
gun like a Tommy his tool
and spray them with its lethal
liquor, after which, I
would arrive with the swatter
and whack the wounded flat,
and those we missed soon
drifted up to the lick-me
stickum unspooling from above,
and once in a while, to my eminent
satisfaction, I would deliberately
leave the door ajar,
just to see my Gran
in action.

Marlene

Marlene Burgess was just
a year older than the girls
who cruised our block, unremarked,
but she had curves where they count
and wind-tossed locks
you could lose your license in,
and when she walked her winsome
body by, no matter how hard
she tried to cosset her urges,
her aftermath wobbled
in ways that galvanized our gaze
and griddled our id, and though
we were far too young to lust,
we did.

Markers

On our mile-and-a-tenth trek
to school each morning,
we passed by five farms
superintended by the Leckies
and their kin, their fields in fallow
or fletched with winter wheat
(that wobbled with the breeze)
or last season's still-cobbed
corn, rusting in the sun,
and I wondered aloud how
the highland clan happened
to set foot upon this
particular untilled, weed-
breeding, God-fearing
ground and put it to the plough,
and laid their marker down –
and soon there were barns and cows
to milk in them and pastures
as green as the glens of Eden –
and they seeded half-a township
with the seething weave of their genes.

Bloodlines

Even with no-one about
to admire the perfect pacing
of his pedigreed lope,
he runs like a thoroughbred
with speed in his genes, just
to feel his legs lengthen
and his hooves pursue their usual
grooves, and the dance of his canter
on the pasture-grass is a
dithyrambic anthem
to muscle in motion, and when
he comes to a stuttering stop
at the meadow's edge, he gives
a stallion's

Voluminous

Easton Burgess, our grocer,
on a sweltering June afternoon,
offers to drop me off home
when he does his distant deliveries,
but first it's time to tickle
his thirst at a regular drinking
den, leaving me to fend
for myself in the parking lot
with two bottles of pop
to keep me amused and in on
the plot, but when an hour
or more, and several pitchers
of froth, have passed indoors,
and I have eased the grief
of the heat nursing Pepsis,
I feel an urge other than
thirst coming on, and find
relief from its helter-skelter
in the only receptacle handy:
Missus Easton's voluminous
purse.

Her Lapdog Eyes

For John

I well remember the day
our Scottie decided to go
for a skate instead of a walk,
and watched, in pedigreed shock,
as the ice gave way beneath
her skidding paws and invited
her in for a wintry swim,
and you, with no thought
but the life of your canine
companion, strode into the
watery waste, plucked up
her soggy deadweight,
tucked her, trembling, under
your coat, and trotted home
slowly to let her breathe
your body-heat and keep
her heart hiccupping, and there
you sat with her, cocooned
in your arms, until at last
she was warm enough to thank you
with her loving, lapdog eyes.

Jewel

For Tom in loving memory

You tried so hard to kick
your addiction, talking even
of someday taking your own
family to Cameron, and showing off
the lake where we spent so many
sun-numbed afternoons,
afloat and free to live
in our skin, and I was sure
that love, like the jewel that makes
the crown, would do the trick,
but you fooled us all –
you died.

Tuck

My father decides it's time
we try our luck angling
in Mitchell's Bay, where the fish
are as thick as Ali Baba's
thieves, and I am appointed
to guide our fifteen-foot
Peterborough and its purring
ten-horse Evinrude
along the meandering, back-
tracking Thames with a deadhead
threatening every bend,
and when we reach the river-
mouth, still afloat
and as tidy as a friar's tuck
(and I give myself a cheer),
the great weed-wracked
bay beckons, where jut-
jawed carnivores cruise
and connive, and here, my Dad
beside, with the sun in love
with light, I am glad to be young
and alive.

Other

In the schoolyard, the girls
were the ones with shocks of hair,
flung free or pinned
pretty, and frilly frocks
the wind dimpled or blew
askew, and bride-white
knee-socks that clung
to calf or gam, and the high-
pitched squeals and ululations
as they gamboled by, just
for the fun of running, their bones
afloat, and the joy of being
bodily buoyant in their long-
legged leaping, not a brow
blemished by sweat or a curl
mussed or mutinous – and all
we ever knew about this
fleeced species: they were
other than us.

Bachelor Bob

Sarnia Township – June: 1949

Bachelor Bob Leckie
steers Coop and me
through the moonless dark
to his new henhouse,
armed with a flashlight
and a hob-nailed bludgeon,
and when he unlatches the door
to let us peer inside,
we spot on the window-ledge
a regimented row of rodents,
their blood-bright sight
blinded by Bob's beam,
and they do not see blows
that knock them senseless
to the feathered floor below,
where they writhe and roil like gutted
geese, until the big barred-
rock cockerel struts up
and plucks at the prize of their dying
eyes, while, behind him,
the nesting hen cluck
their approval and root for the rooster.

Firstborn

Honeymoon Bay: circa 1980
For John

We slept on the grass that girdled
the Bay, under a sky
stencilled with stars, and the slow
peregrination of the moon
thru the arduous dark, lulled
by the lullaby lapping of the lake's
wavelets, and disturbed only
by the shrivelled shrieks of some
woman camper nearby,
too drunk to be unhappy,
but soon the evening soothed
again, and nothing was heard
or noted beyond the demesne
of our dreaming, until another
cry shrilled across the
black bloom of the Bay:
female, feral in its fear,
and eerily familiar, and you dashed
past us, the rescue-ring
already in hand, and plunged
under, stroking your way
towards the witless victim
and her mad thrashing, and my own
uncharitable thought was:
"Don't let her drown you
in her drunken desperation,"
but when you brought her safely
ashore (and got no thanks),
I knew my firstborn was blessed
with the curse of courage.

Angler's Dream

For Tom in loving memory

I so wanted you to live
long enough to catch
a jut-jawed bass
as big as a brigantine,
and savour the smile you'd toss
my way, as wide as Ahab's
gaze when Moby, grazing
for krill to feed his baleen
and brought his great albino
bulk down upon the
bravest wave, and debouched
with the boat and the fool at is tiller,
and O how you loved that sea-
going thriller and the angler's
dream that spawned it:
of landing lunker with a braggart's
bray and a gaff to the gut,
but, like your life, it was the one
that got away.

Rumour

The rumour that Gracie Clair
wore no pants sped
from boy to boy and block
to block, and many a male
who fancied his chances, could be seen
sauntering the walk where Gracie
grew her budding lovelies
and stood amid the flotsam
of her litter-garnished yard,
near nude, and I wondered
what she thought as I passed
her by with a sidelong glance
that said: "There's little joy
in a voyeur's gawk, and not enough
love to go around."

Heart-Healed

Point Edward: 1946

My Grandfather: on his "back forty,"
in the summer-softened sun,
his torso as bronzed as a Benini,
the sweat of his endeavour
burnishing his brow, and this
is the man who spent the green
years of his youth hunched
in the mud and mire of Flanders'
unpoppied fields
and its hand-dug, rain-
drenched trenches (where death
was less than a breath away),
and lived a terror-tugged
month on the Somme when thousands
went down before him to glorify
their king, and here he is:
long home from the Wars,
heart-healed and mowing
lawns.

Once in a While

Once in a while, we paused
from marbles or move-up
long enough to cast
an envious eye across
the walk that kept us gendered,
where the girls played at games
like bounce-a-ball or London
Bridge is falling, chanting
every step of the way,
as if their sing-song
solos might keep the rules
from rupturing or put
more ounce in the bounce,
and O how tame were our taws
and aggies, our cracked bats
and stolen bases, and the guttural
cries we used to announce
our manly mettle and tell
the world how wondrous we were:
and no girl, from her haboured
yard, waved to say,
"Hello, well done."

Duo

For Anne in loving memory

I would not turn away
from love or the swerve of your smile,
even though I know
the chance we take whenever
we leave our hearts open
to hope and happiness, but we are
blood-and-bone beings,
eager to atone for the truancy
of touch, and break the back
of our aloneness —and dance
as a duo to the music of the Muses.

Weightless

It must have been a dream,
but when I woke to let
the day preside, I was certain
I had taken flight, my body
turned awry of the bed
and feeling its bones float
to the brim of the ceiling and out
through the open window,
wingless but lifting aloft
with the joy of being buoyant,
of seeing the world widen
as a bee sees it or an observant
bird, or a poet looking for
the word to best render
the wonder of his weightless state.

When Love Abides

For Anne in loving memory

When love abides, all
else is flotsam, feathering
on the breeze, and when we let
our bodies besot, there is
no need for whether or why-not?
for we are nurtured by the night
and anchored to the dark, where our
dreams ride easy
in the other's sleep, and to wish
ourselves awake from such
a loving slumber, would be
as impolite as a bride's
wedding-night bite.

More than Once

More than once I've dreamt
I could fly, peregrinating
my room an intimate inch
below the ceiling, and reconnoitering
each of the four corners
I knew only from afar,
and hovering above the commode
like a hummingbird on a sugar
high, and whenever tempted
to make a maneuver, all
I had to do was think myself
there and let my bones
elope, and when I woke
to morning's lash of light,
the room was everywhere.

Holy

In the midst of a May morning
I take my daily stroll,
my aging bones assuaged
by the subtleties of the sun, and everything
born to bloom is blooming
now: the serviceberry afloat
in its froth, the cupped loveliness
of a mauve magnolia,
cherry boughs hung
young with snow, forsythia
still thrilling, and the last
of the daffodils casting a golden
glow upon my inward eye,
and I wonder what I have done
in my indifferent decades
to deserve such immutable
beauty – with words enough
to keep it holy.

Ruck

The explosion rattled the glass
of every window in town,
and we rushed, neighbour by neighbour,
towards the dust-cloud
that plumed above the tree-
tops like the aftermath
of some ungodly bomb,
and we arrived to find the Reverend
Bell's manse a smoudering
tangle of brick and plaster-
lath, and the good parson
seated on his manicured grass
as if he were about to give
the Benediction or pass
the plate, and someone said,
"Praised be the Lord,"
but looking, amazed, at the ruin
and ruck, my thought was:
"The Lord was a little late."

Small Betrayals

When my Gran died, the house
where I was weaned, coddled
and lionized for eleven years
was put up for sale, and bought
by the neighbourly Harts, who,
for a friendly price, promised
to keep Grandfather's grounds
intact: with its lilace hedges
that bloomed each June into being,
its rolling green lawns,
the 'back forty' I roamed
like a junior-size LaSalle,
and the two tall trees
that shared their shade with the
front and side verandahs,
but a month after the deed
was done, the neighbourly Harts
severed the lot – and my God
remained in His Heaven.

The Birds and the Bees

I might have been ten
or even eleven when I still
believed the stories of storks
cruising to distant cribs
and married moms, a newborn
slung under their curved
claws, until the day
that Butch took me aside
and explained the laws of the birds
and misbehaving bees
and how they managed the mysteries
of procreation without a
motivating manual
or Heaven's consent.

A Walk Interrupted

When these daffodils
that interrupt my walk begin
to droop, the tulips beside them
gleam more brightly,
as if this season
of bud-bloom and root-
fluming did not remind us
with every flower fletched
or every leaf a-greening
that we are creatures of Time
and Eternity, doomed
to beatify Beauty and watch
it die, while the Earth resumes
its urgent turning.

Translation

I must have been all
of ten when I caught two
dogs 'doing-it' on the walk,
but at the time I thought
they'd simply become in-
cidentally attached, the bigger
one, no relation,
wriggling above the other,
frantic to be free – of what
I wasn't sure until
the girl-next-door,
giggled below her curls
and made a stroke with her fist
that needed no translation.

Bob's Your Uncle

S.S. No. 12 – Sarnia Township
December 1948

In the cloakroom,
Ronnie Young yelps,
"Who cut the cheese?"
and Donny Turnbull, ever
helpful, quips, "Skunk
smells its own hole first,"
and I am bursting to make
a smart remark, but all
that comes to the muddle of my mind
is "Fanny is my aunt and Bob's
your uncle!"

Gravity

We Grade Fives,
feeling ourselves on the cusp
of something, practice the strut
of the bigger boys on campus
and the way they rub their public
parts to signal sexual
savvy, but a giggle and a flippant
sniff from the girls' side
brings us back to Earth
and the grip of is Grade-Five
gravity.

Don Gutteridge was born in Sarnia and raised in the nearby village of Point Edward. He taught High School English for seven years, later becoming a Professor in the Faculty of Education at Western University, where he is now Professor Emeritus. He is the author of more than seventy books: poetry, fiction and scholarly works in pedagogical theory and practice. He has published twenty-two novels, including the twelve-volume Marc Edwards mystery series, and forty-nine books of poetry, one of which, Coppermine, was short-listed for the 1973 Governor-General's Award. In 1970 he won the UWO President's Medal for the best periodical poem of that year, "Death at Quebec." Don lives in London, Ontario.

Email: gutteridgedonald@gmail.com.